Ages 8+

Disney **LEARNING**

Smart S

Multiplication & Division

Carson Dellosa Education
Greensboro, North Carolina

Published by
Carson Dellosa Education
PO Box 35665
Greensboro, NC 27425 USA

Printed in the USA • All rights reserved.
01-053217784

ISBN 978-1-4838-6143-2

Contents

What is Your Name?

This is Finn.
Finn is his name.
Print your name.

Russell

Draw a picture of yourself!

Odd or Even?

Princess Leia and the Rebel Alliance work with helpful droids to fight the Empire. Organize these helpful droids into groups!

2   4

4 is an even number.

Groups that have one left over after they are paired have an odd number.

2   4   5

5 is an odd number.

Count and write the number for each group of droids. Then, label the groups odd or even.

10 even droids

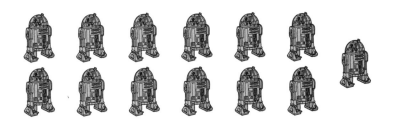

13 odd droids

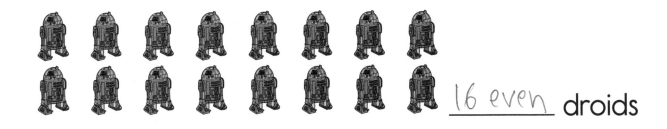

16 even droids

Teaming Up

You multiply when you join equal groups.
Here are 4 groups of 2 rebel starships.

There are **8** rebel starships altogether.

$4 \times 2 = 8$

> This is another way to show the word **multiply**.

Here are groups of rebel starships.

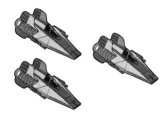  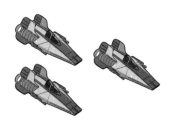

There are rebel starships altogether.

8

Here are 3 groups of 4 rebel starships.

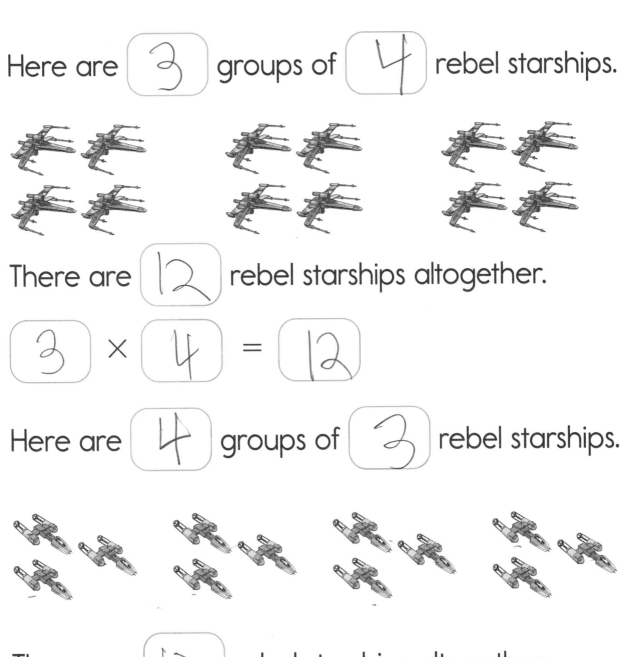

There are 12 rebel starships altogether.

$$3 \times 4 = 12$$

Here are 4 groups of 3 rebel starships.

There are 12 rebel starships altogether.

$$4 \times 3 = 12$$

Learn Together

As your child is being introduced to multiplication, they will still be counting the items within each group to reach a total. Use concrete objects to help them with multiplication as part of this early learning.

Kyber Crystal Problems

Rey trains hard to strengthen her lightsaber skills. Lightsabers need kyber crystals to work. Join equal groups of kyber crystals and try to feel the Force!

Here are groups of kyber crystals.

There are kyber crystals altogether.

 × =

10

Here are groups of kyber crystals.

   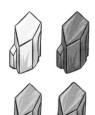

There are kyber crystals altogether.

 × =

Here are groups of kyber crystals.

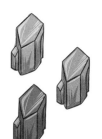  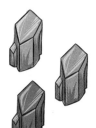  

There are kyber crystals altogether.

 × =

Let's Multiply

The Rebellion is facing a squad of AT-ATs. You can multiply to find out how many they need to take down.

There are **3** groups of **2** AT-ATs.
There are **6** AT-ATs all together.

$$3 \times 2 = 6$$

There are **2** groups of **3** AT-ATs.

$$2 \times 3 = \boxed{}$$

12

There are **6** groups of **2** AT-ATs.

$6 \times 2 =$ ⬚

There are **7** groups of **2** AT-ATs.

$7 \times 2 =$ ⬚

There are **3** groups of **3** AT-ATs.

$3 \times 3 =$ ⬚

Learn Together

Provide your child with other simple scenarios to practice multiplying. Say, "Let's multiply as we set the table. We need 3 sets of 4: 4 plates, 4 knives, and 4 forks. $3 \times 4 = 12$."

Stormtroopers

The Commutative Property says that you can multiply in any order.

4 teams of **3** troopers

$$4 \times 3 = 12$$

$$4 \times 3$$

3 teams of **4** troopers

$$3 \times 4 = 12$$

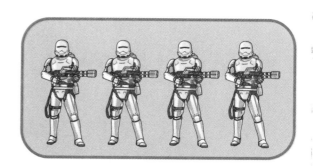

$$=$$

$$3 \times 4$$

14

Use the Commutative Property to complete each math fact.

$5 \times 7 = \underline{} \times \underline{}$

$3 \times 7 = \underline{} \times \underline{}$

$2 \times 9 = \underline{} \times \underline{}$

$3 \times 8 = \underline{} \times \underline{}$

$4 \times 9 = \underline{} \times \underline{}$

$5 \times 8 = \underline{} \times \underline{}$

$5 \times 6 = \underline{} \times \underline{}$

$4 \times 8 = \underline{} \times \underline{}$

Grouping with TIE Fighters

The Associative Property says that when you multiply more than two numbers, you can group the factors in different ways.

Multiply **3 x 2 x 4**.

$(3 \times 2) \times 4$ or $3 \times (2 \times 4)$

6×4 or 3×8

24

You can multiply either way. The product is the same.

Draw parentheses, ( ), to show which factors you multiply first. Then, find the products.

3 x 2 x 2	5 x 2 x 2
$3 \times 2 \times 2$ or $3 \times 2 \times 2$	$5 \times 2 \times 2$ or $5 \times 2 \times 2$
6×2 or 3×4	10×2 or 5×4
_____	_____

4 x 2 x 5

$4 \times 2 \times 5$ or $4 \times 2 \times 5$

8×5 or 4×10

_____

2 x 6 x 2

$2 \times 6 \times 2$ or $2 \times 6 \times 2$

12×2 or 2×12

_____

2 x 3 x 4

$2 \times 3 \times 4$ or $2 \times 3 \times 4$

6×4 or 2×12

_____

4 x 2 x 6

$4 \times 2 \times 6$ or $4 \times 2 \times 6$

8×6 or 4×12

_____

5 x 2 x 3

$5 \times 2 \times 3$ or $5 \times 2 \times 3$

10×3 or 5×6

_____

Adding Up and Multiplying

General Leia Organa is glad to have everyone safe. Use the addition sentences to help you solve the related multiplication sentences.

$9 + 0 = 9$

$1 \times 9 =$ ☐

$4 + 4 = 8$

$4 \times 2 =$ ☐

$3 + 6 = 9$

$3 \times 3 =$ ☐

$5 + 5 = 10$

$5 \times 2 =$ ☐

Use the addition sentences to help you solve the related multiplication sentences.

$3 + 9 = 12$ $3 \times 4 =$ ☐

$2 + 6 = 8$ $2 \times 4 =$ ☐

$8 + 0 = 8$ $8 \times 1 =$ ☐

$2 + 4 = 6$ $2 \times 3 =$ ☐

$4 + 8 = 12$ $4 \times 3 =$ ☐

$0 + 7 = 7$ $1 \times 7 =$ ☐

$2 + 10 = 12$ $2 \times 6 =$ ☐

Learn Together

Help your child to see how each addition sentence is related to a subtraction sentence, and vice versa. Use blocks or toys to show the relationship for one set of sentences.

The Ewoks Are Multiplying!

Multiplication is used to find the total of equal groups.

2 equal groups of 4 Ewoks equals 8 Ewoks

$2 \times 4 = 8$ Ewoks

The Ewoks are everywhere! Finish the multiplication problems to find how many Ewoks have appeared.

$3 \times$ _____ = _____ Ewoks

$4 \times$ _____ = _____ Ewoks

An **array** is a group of objects arranged in equal rows and equal columns. When you multiply, you repeatedly add groups or rows.

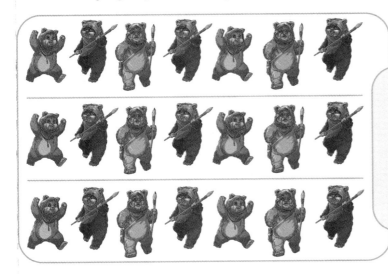

3 rows of 7 Ewoks

equals 21 Ewoks

$7 + 7 + 7 = 21$ Ewoks

$3 \times 7 = 21$

Look at the arrays. Fill in the blanks to complete each problem.

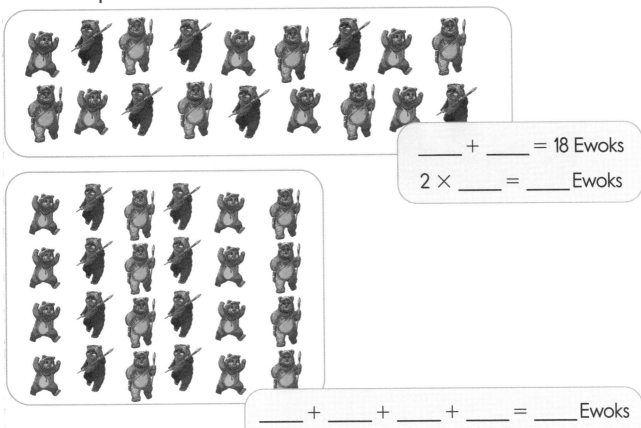

_____ + _____ = 18 Ewoks

$2 \times$ _____ = _____ Ewoks

_____ + _____ + _____ + _____ = _____ Ewoks

_____ $\times$ _____ = _____ Ewoks

Ready, Aim, Fire!

The Resistance and the First Order are engaged in a space battle.

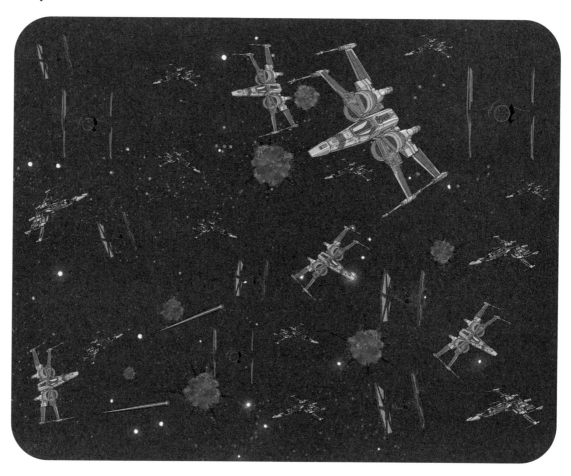

There are **25** ships. How many are left if **10** are shot down?

More ships join, and there are now twice as many as when the battle started. How many ships are there?

Solve each multiplication sentence.

$1 \times 11 =$ ☐ $6 \times 6 =$ ☐

$3 \times 12 =$ ☐ $2 \times 12 =$ ☐

$11 \times 10 =$ ☐ $5 \times 10 =$ ☐

$5 \times 9 =$ ☐ $2 \times 12 =$ ☐

$7 \times 3 =$ ☐ $3 \times 5 =$ ☐

$5 \times 8 =$ ☐ $6 \times 4 =$ ☐

$3 \times 11 =$ ☐ $10 \times 3 =$ ☐

Learn Together

Discuss any patterns your child notices in some of their answers (subtracting 10 from a number means the first digit in the first two-digit number is one less than it was before). They can use those patterns to help them develop strategies for solving problems.

Break the Code

Multiply to find the product.
Use the products to decode the answer to
the question on page 25.

$4 \times 3 =$ _____ Y

$8 \times 5 =$ _____ O

$6 \times 5 =$ _____ N

$3 \times 9 =$ _____ K

$4 \times 9 =$ _____ R

$7 \times 6 =$ _____ E

$9 \times 7 =$ _____ L

$8 \times 7 =$ _____ B

$9 \times 5 =$ _____ A

Question

Which commander of the First Order is also Han Solo and General Leia's son?

Answer

$\overline{}$ $\overline{}$ $\overline{}$ $\overline{}$ $\overline{}$ $\overline{}$ $\overline{}$
27 12 63 40   36 42 30

Stocking Up

Help Finn plan how many boxes of supplies he will need for a mission. Use the multiplication table to find the answers.

number of mission days ⌐

number of supply boxes

×	0	1	2	3	4	5	6	7	8	9	10
0	0	0	0	0	0	0	0	0	0	0	0
1	0	1	2	3	4	5	6	7	8	9	10
2	0	2	4	6	8	10	12	14	16	18	20
3	0	3	6	9	12	15	18	21	24	27	30
4	0	4	8	12	16	20	24	28	32	36	40
5	0	5	10	15	20	25	30	35	40	45	50
6	0	6	12	18	24	30	36	42	48	54	60
7	0	7	14	21	28	35	42	49	56	63	70
8	0	8	16	24	32	40	48	56	64	72	80
9	0	9	18	27	36	45	54	63	72	81	90
10	0	10	20	30	40	50	60	70	80	90	100

factor   3 → Find the number of supply boxes.

factor   ×   5 → Find the number of mission days.

product   1 5 ← The total number of supply boxes where the number of days in mission and the number of suppy boxes meet.

$4 \times 10 =$ ☐

$5 \times 5 =$ ☐

$2 \times 9 =$ ☐

$4 \times 9 =$ ☐

$10 \times 9 =$ ☐

$9 \times 8 =$ ☐

$6 \times 8 =$ ☐

$5 \times 9 =$ ☐

Use the multiplication table on the previous page to find the missing products.

5 × 10 =

7 × 3 =

9 × 6 =

8 × 8 =

4 × 7 =

3 × 10 =

7 × 7 =

6 × 6 =

5 × 9 =

5 × 7 =

3 × 9 =

8 × 9 =

10 × 6 =

10 × 10 =

7 × 5 =

5 × 4 =

One or None

Obi-Wan Kenobi and Anakin Skywalker meet many droids during the Clone Wars. These droids can be different colors.

Write a multiplication fact for the number of red droids in each example. The first one is done for you.

1. $3 \times 0 = 0$

2. _____

3. _____

4. What do you notice when you multiply a number by **0**?

_____

Are blue droids your favorite? Write a a multiplication fact for the number of blue droids in each example.

1. _____

2. _____

3. _____

4.  _____

5. What pattern do you notice when you multiply a number by **1**?

_____

Calculate each multiplication sentence.

1. $41 \times 1 =$ _____

2. $0 \times 420 =$ _____

3. $1 \times 934 =$ _____

Separating Equal Groups

How many groups can **8** rocks be separated into?

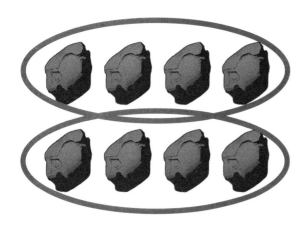

2 groups of 4.

How many groups can **16** rocks be separated into?

groups of 4.

How many groups can **20** rocks be separated into?

$\boxed{}$ groups of **4**.

How many groups can **24** rocks be separated into?

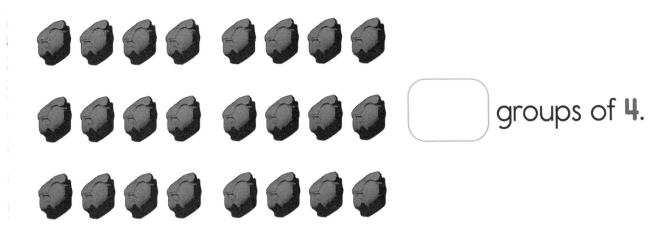

$\boxed{}$ groups of **4**.

Droid Division

When you **divide**, you split a total number of objects into smaller, equal groups. Draw circles around the droids to make equal groups and then fill in the blanks.

Make **3** equal groups.

There are _____ droids in each group.

Make **5** equal groups.

There are _____ droids in each group.

Put **7** droids in each group.

There are _____ groups of 7 droids each.

Put **2** droids in each group.

There are _____ groups of 2 droids each.

Put **3** droids in each group.

There are _____ groups of 3 droids each.

Mission Division

The Resistance has **12** ships ready to go. They are going on **2** different missions. Divide them equally to find out how many to send on each mission.

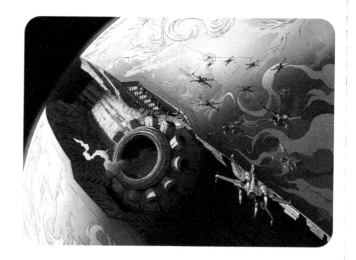

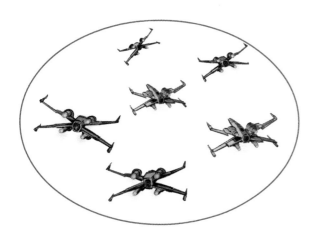

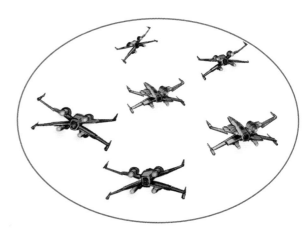

These are two ways to show the word divide.

$$12 \div 2 = 6 \qquad \text{or} \qquad 2 \overline{)12}^{\,6}$$

Circle groups of ships to show each division sentence.

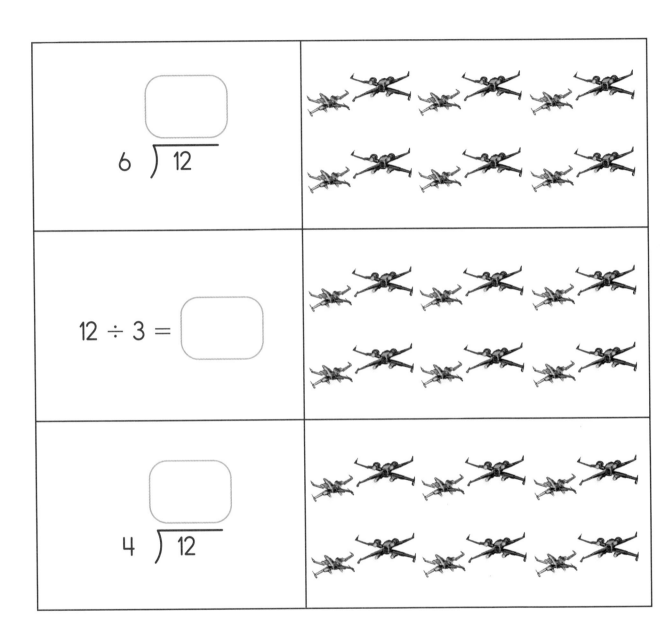

$6 \overline{)12}$

$12 \div 3 = \boxed{}$

$4 \overline{)12}$

Learn Together

Use objects like beads to find the answers and create other problems to solve. The idea of sharing is a familiar one for children, and can help them understand how one group might be divided into smaller equal groups.

Making Equal Groups

The Jedi and their allies work to keep peace in the galaxy.
Split the group of **10** into **2** equal parts.

You have **10** ships and **2, 5,** or **10** bays to keep them in. Using the division sentence, write the number of ships that go in each bay. Then, complete the division sentence.

$$10 \div 2 = \boxed{}$$

$$10 \div 5 = \boxed{}$$

$$10 \div 10 = \boxed{}$$

Break the Code

Divide to find the difference.
Use the differences to decode the answer to
the question on page 39.

$5 \div 5 =$ _____ N

$6 \div 3 =$ _____ M

$8 \div 2 =$ _____ C

$6 \div 1 =$ _____ E

$10 \div 1 =$ _____ L

$9 \div 3 =$ _____ U

$5 \div 1 =$ _____ I

$8 \div 1 =$ _____ F

$9 \div 1 =$ _____ A

$7 \div 1 =$ _____ O

Question

What is the name of
Han Solo's ship?

Answer

$\overline{}$ $\overline{}$ $\overline{}$ $\overline{}$ $\overline{}$ $\overline{}$ $\overline{}$ $\overline{}$ $\overline{}$ $\overline{}$
2   5   10   10   6   1   1   5   3   2

$\overline{}$ $\overline{}$ $\overline{}$ $\overline{}$ $\overline{}$ $\overline{}$
8   9   10   4   7   1

Equal Parties

Luke and Leia are on a mission for the Rebellion. There are **18** people on this mission. They need to check out **2** locations. If the groups are equal, how many rebels should go to each location?

_____

The next mission has **30** people. They need to visit **10** locations. How many rebels should go to each location to keep the groups equal?

_____

The 18 people from the first mission join the 30 people from the second. They divide into equal groups to visit 4 locations. How many people are in each group?

_____

How many groups would there be if each group had 6 people?

_____

All Gone!

If **24** Knights of Ren are divided into groups of **3**, how many groups are there?
Use the chart to find each difference.

1	2	3	4	5	6	7	8	9	10
11	12	13	14	15	16	17	18	19	20
21	22	23	24	25	26	27	28	29	30
31	32	33	34	35	36	37	38	39	40
41	42	43	44	45	46	47	48	49	50

Find each difference.

$$7 \overline{)35}$$

$$10 \overline{)50}$$

$$8 \overline{)32}$$

$$4 \overline{)20}$$

$$4 \overline{)16}$$

$$11 \overline{)22}$$

$$10 \overline{)30}$$

$$3 \overline{)15}$$

$$10 \overline{)20}$$

$$6 \overline{)18}$$

$$8 \overline{)40}$$

$$8 \overline{)32}$$

Learn Together

Discuss any patterns your child notices in some of their answers (subtracting 10 from a number means the first digit in the first two-digit number is one less than it was before). They can use those patterns to help them develop strategies for solving problems.

Find the path through the correct problems to connect Chewbacca with the missing porg.

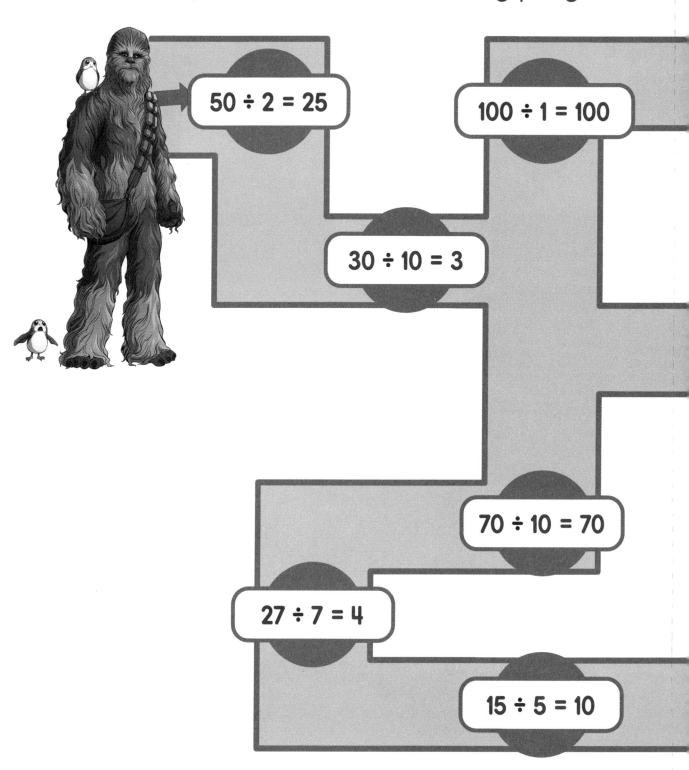

$50 \div 2 = 25$

$100 \div 1 = 100$

$30 \div 10 = 3$

$70 \div 10 = 70$

$27 \div 7 = 4$

$15 \div 5 = 10$

Multiplication & Division © & ™ Lucasfilm Ltd. CD-705393

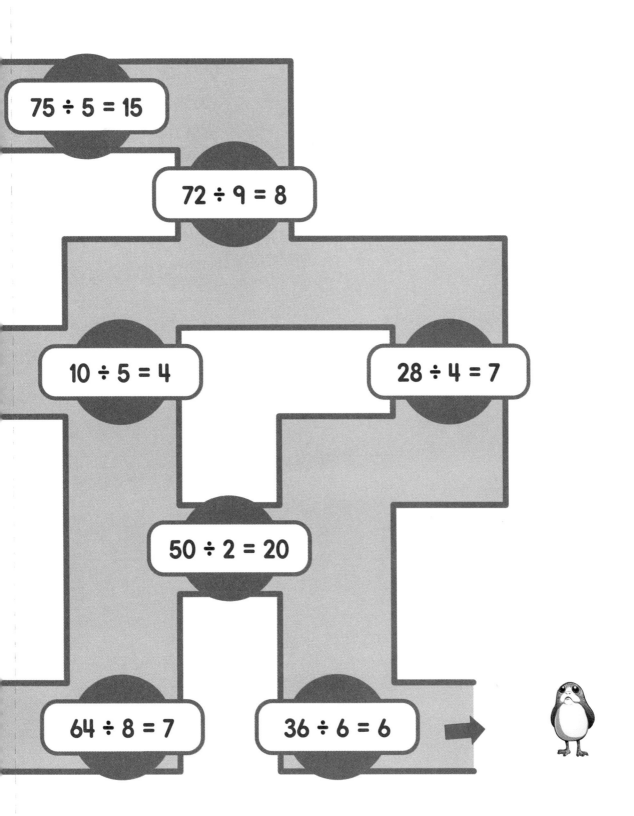

75 ÷ 5 = 15

72 ÷ 9 = 8

10 ÷ 5 = 4

28 ÷ 4 = 7

50 ÷ 2 = 20

64 ÷ 8 = 7

36 ÷ 6 = 6

Divide and Conquer

Rey and Chewbacca see enemy ships! Count the TIE fighters in each example, and write division facts for a number divided by its equal. The first one is done for you.

1. $3 \div 3 = 1$

2. _____

3. _____

4. _____

5. What do you notice when you divide by an equal number?

_____

Poe is a talented pilot who loves flying his X-wing. Write a division fact for the number of ships divided by X-wings.

1.  _____

2. _____

3. _____

4. _____

5. What pattern do you notice when you divide by **1**?

_____

Calculate each division sentence.

1. $7 \div 7 =$ _____

2. $20 \div 1 =$ _____

3. $13 \div 1 =$ _____

Hidden Numbers

A missing number can be anywhere in a division sentence. Use a related multiplication sentence to find the missing number.

$4 \times 5 = 20$, so $20 \div \underline{\hspace{1cm}} = 4$

$\underline{\hspace{1.5cm}} \div 3 = 10$

$40 \div \underline{\hspace{1.5cm}} = 5$

$\underline{\hspace{1.5cm}} \div 6 = 3$

$\underline{\hspace{1.5cm}} \div 7 = 7$

$15 \div \underline{\hspace{1.5cm}} = 3$

$81 \div \underline{\hspace{1.5cm}} = 9$

A missing number can be anywhere in a multiplication number sentence. Use a related division sentence to find the missing number.

$12 \div 3 = 4$, so ___ $\times 4 = 12$

$7 \times$ ___ $= 42$

___ $\times 5 = 10$

___ $\times 12 = 12$

___ $\times 8 = 64$

$9 \times$ ___ $= 54$

$3 \times$ ___ $= 12$

$4 \times$ ___ $= 36$

Creature Word Problems

Read each word problem. Write an equation and then solve the problem.

Reeks have 3 horns on their heads.
How many horns do 5 reeks have in all?

_____ horns

A nexu has 3 claws on each paw. How many claws
will the animal's 4 paws have in all?

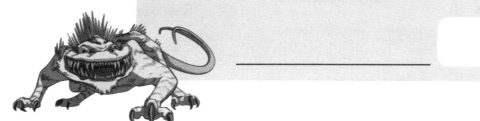

_____ claws

Each rancor has 4 strong limbs.
If you count 24 limbs in all,
how many rancors are there?

_____ rancors

Each acklay has 3 beady eyes. If you see 18 eyes, how many acklay are waiting to pounce?

_____ acklays

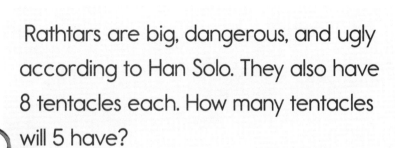

Rathtars are big, dangerous, and ugly according to Han Solo. They also have 8 tentacles each. How many tentacles will 5 have?

_____ tentacles

Gunguns like Jar Jar have 3 toes on each foot and 2 floppy ears. How many ears will 12 Gunguns have?

_____ ears

Missing in Action

Rey is looking for her friends. In multiplication and division, numbers sometimes go missing, too!

Find the missing number for each sentence.

$24 \times \underline{} = 48$

$8 \times \underline{} = 32$

$\underline{} \div 11 = 8$

$\underline{} \div 7 = 1$

$\underline{} \times 11 = 121$

$108 \div \underline{} = 12$

$72 \div \underline{} = 8$

$\underline{} \times 8 = 40$

BB-8 is searching all over the base for Poe. There are **57** rooms, and BB-8 has checked **33** of them. How many are left?

_____

Find the missing number for each sentence.

___ × 11 = 88

11 × ___ = 110

5 × ___ = 50

___ ÷ 9 = 9

___ ÷ 4 = 10

72 ÷ ___ = 12

99 ÷ ___ = 9

6 × ___ = 36

___ × 6 = 48

___ ÷ 12 = 10

Congratulations

to

_____

for completing this workbook!

Keep up the good work!

THE FORCE
IS STRONG
WITH THIS ONE.

Count and write the number for each group of droids. Then, label the groups odd or even.

_10_ droids

even

_13_ droids

odd

_16_ droids

even

Learn Together

Challenge your child to create other multiplication arrays. Encourage them to use 10-frames and counters to help them solve the problem.

7

Teaming Up

You multiply when you join equal groups. Here are 4 groups of 2 rebel starships.

There are 8 rebel starships altogether.

$4 \times 2 = 8$

This is another way to show the word multiply.

Here are [3] groups of [3] rebel starships.

There are [9] rebel starships altogether.

8

Here are [3] groups of [4] rebel starships.

There are [12] rebel starships altogether.

[3] × [4] = [12]

Here are [4] groups of [3] rebel starships.

There are [12] rebel starships altogether.

[4] × [3] = [12]

Learn Together

As your child is being introduced to multiplication, they will still be counting the items within each group to reach a total. Use concrete objects to help them with multiplication as part of this early learning.

9

Kyber Crystal Problems

Rey trains hard to strengthen her lightsaber skills. Lightsabers need kyber crystals to work. Join equal groups of kyber crystals and try to feel the Force!

Here are [5] groups of [2] kyber crystals.

There are [10] kyber crystals altogether.

[5] × [2] = [10]

10

Here are [4] groups of [4] kyber crystals.

There are [16] kyber crystals altogether.

[4] × [4] = [16]

Here are [5] groups of [3] kyber crystals.

There are [15] kyber crystals altogether.

[5] × [3] = [15]

11

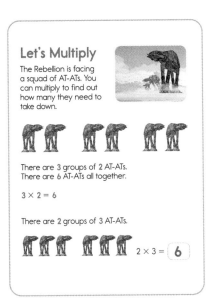

Let's Multiply

The Rebellion is facing a squad of AT-ATs. You can multiply to find out how many they need to take down.

There are 3 groups of 2 AT-ATs.
There are 6 AT-ATs all together.

$3 \times 2 = 6$

There are 2 groups of 3 AT-ATs.

$2 \times 3 =$ **6**

12

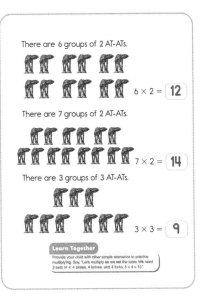

There are 6 groups of 2 AT-ATs.

$6 \times 2 =$ **12**

There are 7 groups of 2 AT-ATs.

$7 \times 2 =$ **14**

There are 3 groups of 3 AT-ATs.

$3 \times 3 =$ **9**

Learn Together

Provide your child with other simple scenarios to practice multiplying. Say, "Let's multiply as we set the table. We need 3 sets of 4: 4 plates, 4 knives, and 4 forks. $3 \times 4 = 12$."

13

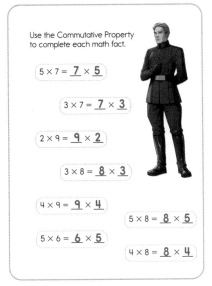

Use the Commutative Property to complete each math fact.

$5 \times 7 =$ **7** $\times$ **5**

$3 \times 7 =$ **7** $\times$ **3**

$2 \times 9 =$ **9** $\times$ **2**

$3 \times 8 =$ **8** $\times$ **3**

$4 \times 9 =$ **9** $\times$ **4**

$5 \times 8 =$ **8** $\times$ **5**

$5 \times 6 =$ **6** $\times$ **5**

$4 \times 8 =$ **8** $\times$ **4**

15

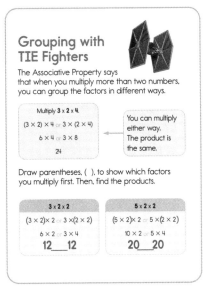

Grouping with TIE Fighters

The Associative Property says that when you multiply more than two numbers, you can group the factors in different ways.

Multiply **3 x 2 x 4**.

$(3 \times 2) \times 4$ or $3 \times (2 \times 4)$

6×4 or 3×8

24

You can multiply either way. The product is the same.

Draw parentheses, ( ), to show which factors you multiply first. Then, find the products.

3 x 2 x 2	5 x 2 x 2
$(3 \times 2) \times 2$ or $3 \times (2 \times 2)$	$(5 \times 2) \times 2$ or $5 \times (2 \times 2)$
6×2 or 3×4	10×2 or 5×4
12 __ 12	**20 __ 20**

16

4 x 2 x 5	2 x 6 x 2
$(4 \times 2) \times 5$ or $4 \times (2 \times 5)$	$(2 \times 6) \times 2$ or $2 \times (6 \times 2)$
8×5 or 4×10	12×2 or 2×12
40 __ 40	**24 __ 24**

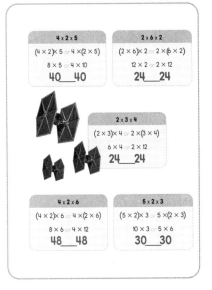

2 x 3 x 4
$(2 \times 3) \times 4$ or $2 \times (3 \times 4)$
6×4 or 2×12
24 __ 24

4 x 2 x 6	5 x 2 x 3
$(4 \times 2) \times 6$ or $4 \times (2 \times 6)$	$(5 \times 2) \times 3$ or $5 \times (2 \times 3)$
8×6 or 4×12	10×3 or 5×6
48 __ 48	**30 __ 30**

17

Adding Up and Multiplying

General Leia Organa is glad to have everyone safe. Use the addition sentences to help you solve the related multiplication sentences.

9 + 0 = 9   1 × 9 = **9**

4 + 4 = 8   4 × 2 = **8**

3 + 6 = 9   3 × 3 = **9**

5 + 5 = 10   5 × 2 = **10**

Use the addition sentences to help you solve the related multiplication sentences.

3 + 9 = 12   3 × 4 = **12**

2 + 6 = 8   2 × 4 = **8**

8 + 0 = 8   8 × 1 = **8**

2 + 4 = 6   2 × 3 = **6**

4 + 8 = 12   4 × 3 = **12**

0 + 7 = 7   1 × 7 = **7**

2 + 10 = 12   2 × 6 = **12**

Learn Together

Help your child to see how each addition sentence is related to a subtraction sentence, and vice versa. Use blocks or toys to show the relationship for one set of sentences.

18

19

The Ewoks Are Multiplying!

Multiplication is used to find the total of equal groups.

2 equal groups of 4 Ewoks equals 8 Ewoks

2 × 4 = 8 Ewoks

The Ewoks are everywhere! Finish the multiplication problems to find how many Ewoks have appeared.

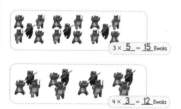

3 × _5_ = _15_ Ewoks

4 × _3_ = _12_ Ewoks

An array is a group of objects arranged in equal rows and equal columns. When you multiply, you repeatedly add groups or rows.

3 rows of 7 Ewoks equals 21 Ewoks

7 + 7 + 7 = 21 Ewoks

3 × 7 = 21

Look at the arrays. Fill in the blanks to complete each addition and multiplication sentence.

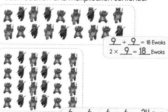

_9_ + _9_ = 18 Ewoks

2 × _9_ = _18_ Ewoks

_6_ + _6_ + _6_ + _6_ = _24_ Ewoks

_4_ × _6_ = _24_ Ewoks

Ready, Aim, Fire!

The Resistance and the First Order are engaged in a space battle.

There are 25 ships. How many are left if 10 are shot down?

15

More ships join, and there are now twice as many as when the battle started. How many ships are there?

50

20

21

22

Solve each multiplication sentence.

$1 \times 11 =$ 11 $6 \times 6 =$ 36

$3 \times 12 =$ 36 $2 \times 12 =$ 24

$11 \times 10 =$ 110 $5 \times 10 =$ 50

$5 \times 9 =$ 45 $2 \times 12 =$ 24

$7 \times 3 =$ 21 $3 \times 5 =$ 15

$5 \times 8 =$ 40 $6 \times 4 =$ 24

$3 \times 11 =$ 33 $10 \times 3 =$ 30

Learn Together

Discuss any patterns your child notices in some of their answers (subtracting 10 from a number means the first digit in the first two-digit number is one less than it was before). They can use those patterns to help them develop strategies for solving problems.

23

Break the Code

Multiply to find the product.
Use the products to decode the answer to the question on page 25.

$4 \times 3 =$ 12 Y

$8 \times 5 =$ 40 O

$6 \times 5 =$ 30 N

$3 \times 9 =$ 27 K

$4 \times 9 =$ 36 R

$7 \times 6 =$ 42 E

$9 \times 7 =$ 63 L

$8 \times 7 =$ 56 B

$9 \times 5 =$ 45 A

24

Question
Which commander of the First Order is also Han Solo and General Leia's son?

Answer

K   Y   L   O   R   E   N
27   12   63   40   36   42   30

25

Stocking Up

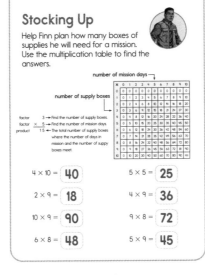

Help Finn plan how many boxes of supplies he will need for a mission. Use the multiplication table to find the answers.

number of mission days →

number of supply boxes →

factor   3 → Find the number of supply boxes.
factor   × 5 → Find the number of mission days.
product 1 5 ← The total number of supply boxes where the number of days in mission and the number of supply boxes meet.

$4 \times 10 =$ 40 $5 \times 5 =$ 25

$2 \times 9 =$ 18 $4 \times 9 =$ 36

$10 \times 9 =$ 90 $9 \times 8 =$ 72

$6 \times 8 =$ 48 $5 \times 9 =$ 45

26

Use the multiplication table on the previous page to find the missing products.

$5 \times 10 =$ 50 $7 \times 3 =$ 21

$9 \times 6 =$ 54 $8 \times 8 =$ 64

$4 \times 7 =$ 28 $3 \times 10 =$ 30

$7 \times 7 =$ 49 $6 \times 6 =$ 36

$5 \times 9 =$ 45 $5 \times 7 =$ 72

$3 \times 9 =$ 27 $8 \times 9 =$ 72

$10 \times 6 =$ 60 $10 \times 10 =$ 100

$7 \times 5 =$ 35 $5 \times 4 =$ 20

27

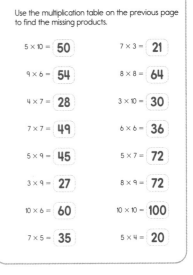

One or None

Obi-Wan Kenobi and Anakin Skywalker meet many droids during the Clone Wars. These droids can be different colors.

Write a multiplication fact for the number of red droids in each example. The first one is done for you.

1. $3 \times 0 = 0$
2. $4 \times 0 = 0$
3. $7 \times 0 = 0$

4. What do you notice when you multiply a number by 0?

The product is always 0.

28

Are blue droids your favorite? Write a a multiplication fact for the number of blue droids in each example.

1. $1 \times 1 = 1$
2. $3 \times 1 = 3$
3. $5 \times 1 = 5$
4. $7 \times 1 = 7$

5. What pattern do you notice when you multiply a number by 1?
When you multiply any number by 1, the product remains the original number.

Calculate each multiplication sentence.

1. $41 \times 1 =$ __41__
2. $0 \times 420 =$ __0__
3. $1 \times 934 =$ __934__

29

Separating Equal Groups

How many groups can 8 rocks be separated into?

 __2__ groups of 4.

How many groups can 16 rocks be separated into?

 __4__ groups of 4.

30

How many groups can 20 rocks be separated into?

 __5__ groups of 4.

How many groups can 24 rocks be separated into?

 __6__ groups of 4.

Learn Together

Your child is just being introduced to the concept of division. Help your child solve these problems. Provide them with counters to arrange into groups of 4.

31

Droid Division

When you divide, you split a total number of objects into smaller, equal groups. Draw circles around the droids to make equal groups and then fill in the blanks.

Make 3 equal groups.

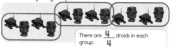

There are __4__ droids in each group.

Make 5 equal groups.

There are __3__ droids in each group.

32

Put 7 droids in each group.

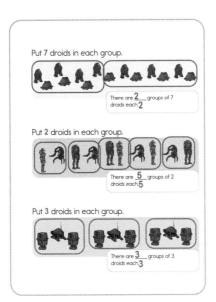

There are _2_ groups of 7
droids each. 2

Put 2 droids in each group.

There are _5_ groups of 2
droids each. 5

Put 3 droids in each group.

There are _3_ groups of 3
droids each. 3

33

(Circle) groups of ships to show
each division sentence.

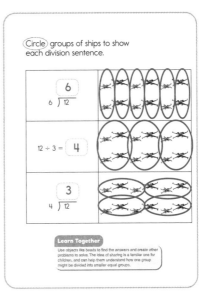

$$\boxed{6}$$
$$6\overline{)12}$$

$$12 \div 3 = \boxed{4}$$

$$\boxed{3}$$
$$4\overline{)12}$$

Learn Together
Use objects like beads to find the answers and create other
problems to solve. The idea of sharing is a familiar one for
children, and can help them understand how one group
might be divided into smaller equal groups.

35

Making Equal Groups

The Jedi and their allies work to keep peace in
the galaxy.
Split the group of 10 into 2 equal parts.

36

You have 10 ships and 2, 5, or 10 bays to keep
them in. Using the division sentence, write the
number of ships that go in each bay. Then,
complete the division sentence.

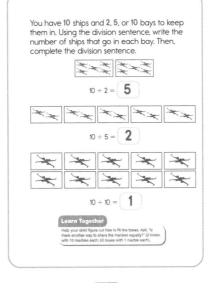

$$10 \div 2 = \boxed{5}$$

$$10 \div 5 = \boxed{2}$$

$$10 \div 10 = \boxed{1}$$

Learn Together
Help your child figure out how to fill the boxes. Ask, "Is
there another way to share the marbles equally?" (2 boxes
with 10 marbles each; 20 boxes with 1 marble each).

37

Break the Code

Divide to find the difference.
Use the differences to decode the answer to
the question on page 39.

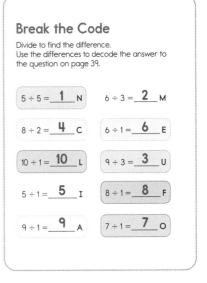

$$5 \div 5 = \underline{1}\ \text{N} \qquad 6 \div 3 = \underline{2}\ \text{M}$$

$$8 \div 2 = \underline{4}\ \text{C} \qquad 6 \div 1 = \underline{6}\ \text{E}$$

$$10 \div 1 = \underline{10}\ \text{L} \qquad 9 \div 3 = \underline{3}\ \text{U}$$

$$5 \div 1 = \underline{5}\ \text{I} \qquad 8 \div 1 = \underline{8}\ \text{F}$$

$$9 \div 1 = \underline{9}\ \text{A} \qquad 7 \div 1 = \underline{7}\ \text{O}$$

38

39

Question
What is the name of Han Solo's ship?

Answer

$$\underset{2}{M} \; \underset{5}{I} \; \underset{10}{L} \; \underset{10}{L} \; \underset{6}{E} \; \underset{1}{N} \; \underset{1}{N} \; \underset{5}{I} \; \underset{3}{U} \; \underset{2}{M}$$

$$\underset{8}{F} \; \underset{9}{A} \; \underset{10}{L} \; \underset{4}{C} \; \underset{7}{O} \; \underset{1}{N}$$

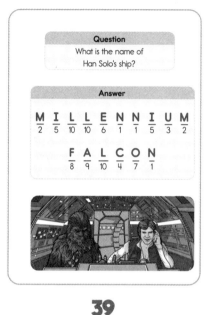

40

Equal Parties

Luke and Leia are on a mission for the Rebellion. There are 18 people on this mission. They need to check out 2 locations. If the groups are equal, how many rebels should go to each location?

9

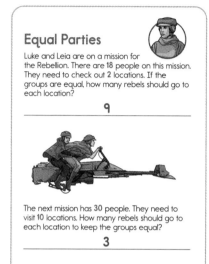

The next mission has 30 people. They need to visit 10 locations. How many rebels should go to each location to keep the groups equal?

3

41

The 18 people from the first mission join the 30 people from the second. They divide into equal groups to visit 4 locations. How many people are in each group?

12

How many groups would there be if each group had 6 people?

8

43

Find each difference.

$7\overline{)35} = 5$ $10\overline{)50} = 5$ $8\overline{)32} = 4$

$4\overline{)20} = 5$ $4\overline{)16} = 4$ $11\overline{)22} = 2$

$10\overline{)30} = 3$ $3\overline{)15} = 5$ $10\overline{)20} = 2$

$6\overline{)18} = 3$ $8\overline{)40} = 5$ $8\overline{)32} = 4$

Learn Together

Discuss any patterns your child notices in some of their answers (subtracting 10 from a number means the first digit in the first two-digit number is one less than it was before). They can use those patterns to help them develop strategies for solving problems.

44

Find the path through the correct problems to connect Chewbacca with the missing porg.

$50 \div 2 = 25$

$100 \div \; = 100$

$30 \div 10 = 3$

$70 \div 10 = 70$

$27 \div 7 = 4$

$15 \div 5 = 10$

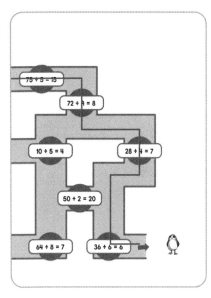

45

Divide and Conquer

Rey and Chewbacca see enemy ships! Count the TIE fighters in each example, and write division facts for a number divided by its equal. The first one is done for you.

HHH 1. $\underline{3 \div 3 = 1}$ _____

HHHH 2. $\underline{4 \div 4 = 1}$ _____

HH 3. $\underline{2 \div 2 = 1}$ _____

HHHH
HHH 4. $\underline{7 \div 7 = 1}$ _____

5. What do you notice when you divide by an equal number?
$\underline{\text{The product is always 1.}}$

46

Poe is a talented pilot who loves flying his X-wing. Write a division fact for the number of ships divided by X-wings.

1. ✈ $\underline{1 \div 1 = 1}$ _____

2. H H ✈ $\underline{3 \div 1 = 2}$ _____

3. H H H ✈ H $\underline{5 \div 1 = 5}$ _____

4. ✈HHHHHHH $\underline{8 \div 1 = 8}$ _____

5. What pattern do you notice when you divide by 1?
When you divide any number by 1,
$\underline{\text{the product remains the original number.}}$

Calculate each division sentence.

1. $7 \div 7 = \underline{1}$
2. $20 \div 1 = \underline{20}$
3. $13 \div 1 = \underline{13}$

47

Hidden Numbers

A missing number can be anywhere in a division sentence. Use a related multiplication sentence to find the missing number.

$4 \times 5 = 20$, so $20 \div \underline{\hspace{0.5cm}} = 4$

$\underline{30} \div 3 = 10$

$40 \div \underline{8} = 5$

$\underline{18} \div 6 = 3$

$\underline{49} \div 7 = 7$

$15 \div \underline{5} = 3$

$81 \div \underline{9} = 9$

48

A missing number can be anywhere in a multiplication number sentence. Use a related division sentence to find the missing number.

$12 \div 3 = 4$, so $\underline{\hspace{0.5cm}} \times 4 = 12$

$7 \times \underline{6} = 42$

$\underline{2} \times 5 = 10$

$\underline{1} \times 12 = 12$

$\underline{8} \times 8 = 64$

$9 \times \underline{6} = 54$

$3 \times \underline{4} = 12$

$4 \times \underline{9} = 36$

49

Creature Word Problems

Read each word problem. Write an equation and then solve the problem.

Reeks have 3 horns on their heads. How many horns do 5 reeks have in all?

$5 \times 3 = n$ 15 horns

A nexu has 3 claws on each paw. How many claws will the animal's 4 paws have in all?

$3 \times 4 = n$ 12 claws

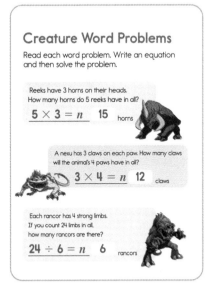

Each rancor has 4 strong limbs. If you count 24 limbs in all, how many rancors are there?

$24 \div 6 = n$ 6 rancors

50

Each acklay has 3 beady eyes. If you see 18 eyes, how many acklay are waiting to pounce?

$18 \div 3 = n$ 6 acklays

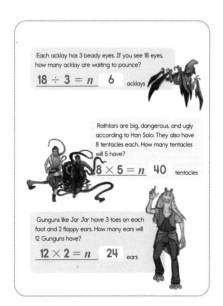

Rathtars are big, dangerous, and ugly according to Han Solo. They also have 8 tentacles each. How many tentacles will 5 have?

$8 \times 5 = n$ 40 tentacles

Gunguns like Jar Jar have 3 toes on each foot and 2 floppy ears. How many ears will 12 Gunguns have?

$12 \times 2 = n$ 24 ears

51

Missing in Action

Rey is looking for her friends. In multiplication and division, numbers sometimes go missing, too!

Find the missing number for each sentence.

$24 \times \underline{2} = 48$ $8 \times \underline{4} = 32$

$\underline{88} \div 11 = 8$ $\underline{7} \div 7 = 1$

$\underline{11} \times 11 = 121$ $108 \div \underline{9} = 12$

$72 \div \underline{9} = 8$ $\underline{5} \times 8 = 40$

52

BB-8 is searching all over the base for Poe. There are 57 rooms, and BB-8 has checked 33 of them. How many are left?

24

Find the missing number for each sentence.

$\underline{8} \times 11 = 88$ $11 \times \underline{10} = 110$

$5 \times \underline{10} = 50$ $\underline{81} \div 9 = 9$

$\underline{40} \div 4 = 10$ $72 \div \underline{6} = 12$

$99 \div \underline{11} = 9$ $6 \times \underline{6} = 36$

$\underline{8} \times 6 = 48$ $\underline{120} \div 12 = 10$

53